Ants Work Best Together

31 Object Lessons from Nature

Joy Gee

CSS Publishing Company, Inc., Lima, Ohio

ANTS WORK BEST TOGETHER

Copyright © 2007 by
CSS Publishing Company, Inc.
Lima, Ohio

All rights reserved. No part of this publication may be reproduced in any manner whatsoever without the prior permission of the publisher, except in the case of brief quotations embodied in critical articles and reviews. Inquiries should be addressed to: Permissions, CSS Publishing Company, Inc., 517 South Main Street, Lima, Ohio 45804.

Some scripture quotations are from the Revised Standard Version of the Bible, copyrighted 1946, 1952 ©, 1971, 1973 by the Division of Christian Education of the National Council of the Churches of Christ in the USA. Used by permission.

Library of Congress Cataloging-in-Publication Data

Gee, Joy.
   Ants work best together : 31 object lessons from nature / Joy Gee.
     p. cm.
   ISBN 0-7880-2411-6 (perfect bound : alk paper)
   1. Object-teaching. 2. Christian education—Teaching methods. 3. Nature—Religious aspects—Christianity. I. Title.
   BV1536.5.G44 2007
268'.432—dc22

2006031565

For more information about CSS Publishing Company resources, visit our website at www.csspub.com or email us at custserv@csspub.com or call (800) 241-4056.

Cover design by Barbara Spencer
ISBN-13: 978-0-7880-2411-5
ISBN-10: 0-7880-2411-6

PRINTED IN U.S.A.

*To my Heavenly Father
and my earthly father.
One made the trees.
The other taught me to hug them.*

Table Of Contents

Introduction   7

Series Sermons   11
  Ants   15
    Don't Get Weary Of Doing Good   17
    Treasures In Heaven   19
    Together   20
    Following   21

  Frogs   25
    The Power Of The Tongue   27
    Change For Better Or Worse   28
    Looking To Jesus   29
    Praise Joyfully   31

  Butterflies   35
    The Eye Of Faith   37
    Growing By The Word Of God   38
    Is He Dead?   39
    Ascending To Heaven   40

  Grass   43
    What Kind Of Soil?   45
    Sowing A Seed   47
    Weeds!   48
    Water!   50

Single Sermons   53
  Don't Be Ashamed   55
  The Armor Of God   56
  Pray, Pray, Pray   58
  Walk In The Light   59

Hold On To The Good	60
Run!	61
Superman!	62
Don't Be Lukewarm	63
Under His Shadow	64
Sweet Like Honey	65
Hearing The Voice Of God	66
Hang In There	67

Other Objects 71
   In Him 73
   What Are You Building? 75
   God Looks At The Heart 76

Conclusion 79

Introduction

Nothing livens up a Sunday school or children's church like something alive! This is why I began using small animals, insects, and other natural objects to teach Bible truths to very young children. I tried these sermonettes and object lessons first on the three-year-olds in my preschool class. Later, I expanded the same outlines for use with children up to late elementary school age. Almost every lesson on these pages has been field tested on at least two different age groups. These are not all the lessons I have, but these are the best!

Before seeking publication, I presented some of these object lessons at a west coast conference of the Association of Christian Schools International. They were well received and generally praised. The next spring, I received remarks from those who had attended the seminar and taken the materials to try in their own classes. Everyone reported success.

With that encouragement under my belt, I offer them to you. I believe with all my heart that God intended his creation to be a witness of his love and the plan he has for our lives. As educators, we have been given a wonderful tool. Let us educate ourselves so that we may better use it.

This is our Father's world. What a world it is when we explore it with the eyes of a child!

In Christ,
Joy Gee

Series Sermons

Young children learn best from repetition and rehearsal. It is difficult sometimes, especially if you only have your group once a week, to give children the repetition necessary to make an idea stick. Live object lessons help to solve this problem. By bringing the same classroom visitor several weeks in a row, we give the children an opportunity to refresh their memories about the previous lessons involving that object. Think about it. Which of these openings is more likely to get a response from the children in your class?

Who can tell me what we talked about last week? *(Likely response: Do you even remember?)*

or

Look, boys and girls, I brought my puppy again today! Does anyone remember what this cute, little puppy taught us about God last week?

With this in mind, I developed a number of series sermons. These will allow you to use the same live object for four different lessons over the course of a month. You will be amazed how these clever classroom visitors enhance your children's ability to retain the life-changing information you are imparting to them!

And please! Don't stick to the script! Let your creative anointing and acting skills flow with the subject. The children will be delighted when they see how much you are enjoying yourself! Joy is, after all, contagious.

Ants

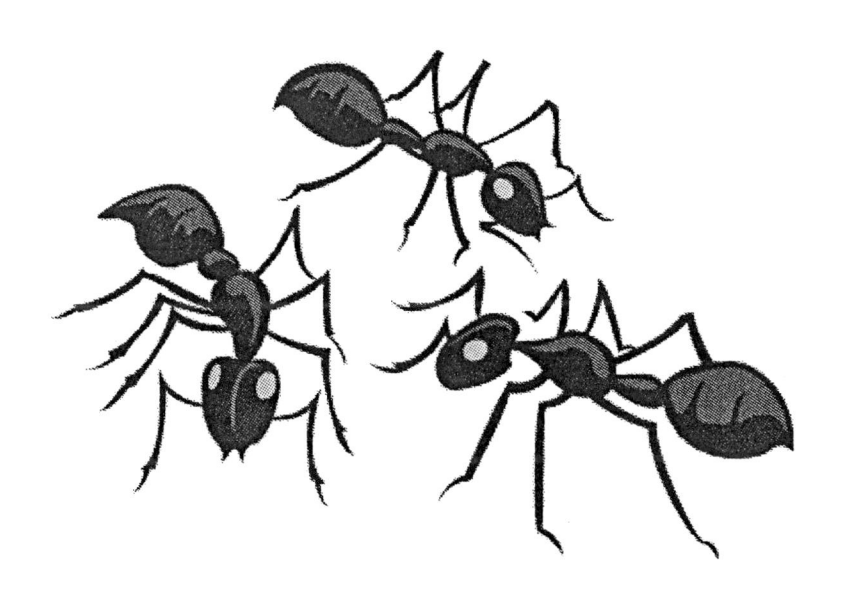

Ants make great classroom visitors for the beginner because they are quiet, interesting, readily available, and fairly easy to transport. Ants and ant farms can be purchased online or at your neighborhood toy and hobby shop. If you are on a tight budget, you can make your own farm and capture your own ants. Both ways work fine.

Commercial ant farms come with instructions and a coupon for ordering ants. The ants can take quite a while to arrive, so if you order them, plan your lessons for about six to eight weeks in the future. You may capture your own ants, of course, but make sure they are the large ones or they will escape from the ventilation holes!

To make your own little ant farm, simply place a small jar inside a large one. Be sure the large jar has clear sides for viewing the ants. Fill the space between the two jars with damp sand or special ant farm medium. I don't recommend potting soil because it coats the walls of the jar and makes viewing difficult. Also, the dark color of the soil hides the ants. Leave at least two inches of space at the top for the ants to make a hill and screw a lid onto the large jar. You can punch a few holes in the lid if you like, or you can just open the jar twice a day to give the ants fresh air. They will be livelier with the holes, but you might lose them if they are small enough to squeeze through.

Order your ants from a supplier online or capture some from the yard. The best way to capture them is to find an anthill or trail, then place a stick among the ants. Several individuals will probably climb the stick and you can shake them gently into your ant farm. Give your ants a drop of sugar water every few days and a crumb or two of food. Any kind of food will do, but choose things that do not mold easily.

Transport the ants carefully. They don't like earthquakes! They should do fine going back and forth to church several times, though. The sand will stay damp and will not collapse on them unless the shaking is pretty severe. Don't let the children hold the ant farm, however. The temptation to shake is just too great! If you have a small class, you can set the ants on a table while you talk about them and then let the children observe them with magnifying glasses.

Ants are quiet. They don't have any noticeable odor, and you don't have to clean up after them. And when your lesson is done, just dump any surviving ants outside. I always think disposable pets are best, don't you?

Don't Get Weary Of Doing Good

Scripture: Galatians 6:9
So let us not grow weary in doing what is right, for we will reap at harvest time, if we did not give up.

Material: an ant farm; this can be a nice one from the store, or you can make your own by placing a small jar inside a large one and filling the space between the two with moist sand. Put a tight lid with a few very small air holes on the larger jar after you add the ants.

Let's see what we have today ... ants! How many of you guys have seen ants out in your yard or on the playground? How many of you have seen ants in your house? *(insert some personal adventure involving an ant invasion of your home or someone else's ... we've all had them)*

But I'm not going to let these ants out of the jar today. I'm going to let them visit with us from right in there and then take them back to their anthill after class, okay?

Have you ever noticed how small ants are? Each one of them is so tiny! And if you watch them working, even in an ant farm like this one, you can see that each one of them takes one grain of sand and moves it. Then they go back for another grain of sand and another. I have even sneaked down at night and shined a flashlight on these guys, and do you know what? They are still working. They just don't quit.

Now, moving one grain of sand at a time might not seem like a big deal, but after a while, these ants will have tunnels and storage rooms all through this jar. If they were outside, where they could just keep digging, their tunnels might run for a mile or more! *(give an illustration of some local landmark to show them how far that is)* Isn't that amazing? And in some parts of the world, ants build huge towers out of the soil they carry up: towers as tall as a grown man! *(use your hand to indicate the height of an adult, or point out a tall person in the congregation)*

You know what, boys and girls? Sometimes you might think you are really small, like these ants. And you might think that the things you can do are small, too; things like being kind to your friends, giving in the offering, and praying for your pastor. But if you just keep doing the little things you can do, it's like moving sand one grain at a time. Pretty soon you have gone a long, long way and built a high, high tower. Just like the ants, you can do it one act of kindness, one gift, and one prayer at a time.

Treasures In Heaven

Scripture: Matthew 6:19-20
Do not store up for yourselves treasures on earth, where moth and rust consume and where thieves break in and steal; but store up for yourselves treasures in heaven, where neither moth nor rust consumes and where thieves do not break in and steal.

Material: ant farm

Look at this, boys and girls. I brought the ant farm again, and what do you think? Our friend ants have been working and working. Even though they are very small, these ants have moved one grain of sand after another until they have built up quite a little city here. Look how much sand they have piled up at the top of their little anthills. I can see tunnels and rooms and ... look! They are storing all kinds of food down in those tunnels!

Who can tell me what ants might want to store in their tunnels? *(look into the ant farm every now and then to keep pulling the children's attention back to it as you discuss what ants might store in the tunnels; as an added object, you could have samples of the foods you have been feeding the ants, such as seeds, bread crumbs, or bits of cracker)* I think we can all learn a lesson from the ants. They tell us it is important to store things up.

What about you, boys and girls? If you had a secret tunnel, what would you store in it? *(allow more discussion, but try to get the word "treasure")*

But you know what? God tells us to store things in a special way. He says we should be storing up our treasures in heaven, and the kind of treasure you can store in heaven is the good things you do while you are here on this earth. So pray and read your Bible. Be kind to others and give. These are the treasures that can be stored in heaven, and that is better than any secret tunnel!

Together

Scripture: Matthew 6:19-20
> *Do not store up for yourselves treasures on earth, where moth and rust consume and where thieves break in and steal; but store up for yourselves treasures in heaven, where neither moth nor rust consumes and where thieves do not break in and steal.*

Material: one ant farm with ants and one without ants

I brought my friendly ants again this week! I think they are good Sunday school teachers, don't you? They have already taught us that we can get a lot done if we just keep doing one little bit at a time. And they taught us that we can store up treasure in heaven. I wonder what we can learn from them today? *(look at the ants).*

Hmmmm. I was wondering. What would happen if I took one of these little ants out of here and put him in an ant farm all alone? *(open the ant farm and use a stick to move one ant from the community farm to the other farm)* Would he be able to dig long tunnels? *(point out some tunnels in the community ant farm and then look at the one with just one ant, then shake your head sadly)*

Would he be able to form big piles of sand? *(indicate the piles of sand at the top of the community farm, then look at the other farm and shake your head sadly, again)*

Would one little ant, all alone, be able to store up treasures in his tunnels like these little fellows have? No, I don't think so. One little ant all alone might be able to dig a short tunnel ... and pile up a little hill of sand ... and store a little food. But God made it so that ants work best when they work together.

He made us that way, too. He wants us to worship together, to learn together, and to pray together ... just like we are doing in church this morning. He doesn't want any of us to be like a little ant, all alone.

You know something else? Jesus says that we get together because we love him; he is there, too.

Following

Scripture: Exodus 23:2
You shall not follow a majority in wrongdoing; when you bear witness in a lawsuit, you shall not side with the majority so as to pervert justice.

Material: ant farm

Hi, boys and girls. This is our last week to talk about our little friends the ants. *(indicate ant farm)* We have learned so much from these little guys! Through the ants, God has shown us that we can get a lot done if we just don't quit, and if we work together. He has also taught us to store up our treasures in heaven. Today I want you to notice one more thing about ants.

Do you know that song that goes, "the ants go marching one by one"? *(sing the song)* Well, when I see ants, especially the ones who are marching along in my kitchen, I always see them in a trail. They walk one behind the other. They don't go over this way *(demonstrate by wandering around the front of the room)*, or over that way. *(more wandering)* They follow right along in a line. *(march across the front of the room)* Sometimes they meet some ants that are coming back along the trail and they take their little antennae and go like this. *(imitate an ant with your hands on your forehead like antennae)* But they stay right on their trail, don't they? Every ant follows the other. In fact, you can walk back along the ant trail and find out where they are coming from, like this. *(imitate following an ant trail along the wall or floor)*

Following is good. These ants follow each other to find food and to know where to work. We should follow, too. We should follow Jesus, our parents, our teachers, and our good Christian friends. If we follow good examples, we will get to where we want to go.

There is a different kind of following that is not good. Sometimes we are tempted to follow a bad example. Sometimes we want to do something that we know is not right just because we see everybody else doing it! Let's learn a lesson from the ants and follow after a good example, not a bad one.

Frogs

In most places it is legal to keep a captured frog for a time if the purpose is educational. I have never had anyone complain about me temporarily keeping a native frog for classroom use, but if you have qualms about it, check the internet for regulations in your area. As a last resort, you can order tadpoles from classroom suppliers and grow your own local frogs, or you can purchase any of a number of exotic frogs from pet stores. Keep in mind, though, that nonnative species must *not* be released into the wild. Store-bought frogs are therefore not disposable. It is far easier to visit a local bog and use a butterfly or fishing net to capture your own, then you can release them again when you are done with your lesson series.

Frogs are easy to maintain in the short term. Almost all frogs will eat crickets quite readily if they are fed live about twice or three times a week. It's a little strange to some people, but I have been known to do a lesson on crickets and then one on frogs. This allows me to dispose of one set of classroom visitors by feeding them to the next! Hey, it's nature! Simply provide your froggy friend with a container that allows him to enter water (dechlorinated!) or get out of it onto a stick or other platform. This habitat will do for a month. They don't need anything fancier unless you are planning to keep them longer.

Handle frogs carefully. They are slippery in your hand and can leap farther than you think. This is part of their fascination! Children should not be allowed to pet the frogs as they may be carrying bacteria.

The Power Of The Tongue

Scripture: Proverbs 18:21
Death and life are in the power of the tongue, and those who love it will eat its fruits.

Material: a frog

Our visitor in class this morning is this cute little frog. *(describe the frog, his coloring, how you came to have him, and so on)* His name is _____. *(children relate better to the less usual animals if they have names)*

Frogs are very handy to have around. Do you know why? It's because of what they eat. Frogs eat lots of flies and mosquitoes and other biting bugs that we don't like. They also eat crickets and grasshoppers and mealworms. And frogs don't stop there! *(let your voice get more and more excited)* Frogs eat regular earthworms, beetles, butterflies, moths, dragonflies, crane flies, lacewings ... and even other frogs. As a matter of fact, frogs will eat just about anything that moves and will fit down their throats.

How do they do it? Well, here is the trick. Frogs have tongues that flick way, way out of their mouths. So when Mr. Frog sees a tasty bug ... or his tasty neighbor frog ... he just *flicks* his sticky tongue out there and catches him. Then, gobble-gobble down the throat, and it is done. Yes, old Mr. Frog can do a lot of damage with his tongue.

You know who else can do a lot of damage with a tongue? You can. You and you and me. The Bible says that death and life are in the power of the tongue. We can use our tongues to hurt people, or to help people. No, we don't do it by flicking our tongues out and eating our neighbors like the frog. We do it by flicking our tongues out and saying unkind and hurtful words. Let's learn from the frog, and use our tongues only for life.

Change For Better Or For Worse

Scripture: 1 Corinthians 15:33
Do not be deceived: "Bad company ruins good morals."

Material: a frog, a tadpole, or pictures of a frog and tadpole

Look, boys and girls, I brought our friendly frog back to visit with us again.

Did you know that frogs *(show frog or frog picture)* grow from tadpoles? *(show tadpole or tadpole picture)* Yes, they do! It happens very gradually. The little tadpole is swimming around eating his algae in the pond when he starts to grow legs. His legs get bigger and bigger and his tail gets smaller and smaller. Finally, after a long time, the little frog has no tail at all and four nice legs just made for hopping. Hop — hop — hop. Now I would call that a change for the better! Now he is not stuck in the pond anymore. He can come and go whenever he wants to.

But there is another change that can happen to frogs. Did you know that some frogs, especially tree frogs, change color to match the place where they live? That's right. A tree frog that sits on a green leaf will turn green. If he sits on a brown branch he will turn brown. That's good, because it keeps the frog safe. It's called camouflage: blending in with the surroundings.

People change, too. We change to match whatever kind of friends we stay with most of the time. If we spend most of our time with Christian friends who know how to live for Jesus, we will become more like them. If we spend most of our time with people who behave badly, we will also begin to behave badly as we become more like them.

Let's take a lesson from the frog and remember that we will change to blend in with our surroundings. We need to surround ourselves with good, Christian friends.

Looking To Jesus

Scripture: Acts 3:1-8; Romans 1:20

One day Peter and John were going up to the temple at the hour of prayer, at three o'clock in the afternoon. And a man lame from birth was being carried in. People would lay him daily at the gate of the temple called the Beautiful Gate so that he could ask for alms from those entering the temple. When he saw Peter and John about to go into the temple, he asked them for alms. Peter looked intently at him, as did John, and said, "Look at us." And he fixed his attention on them, expecting to receive something from them. But Peter said, "I have no silver or gold, but what I have I give you; in the name of Jesus Christ of Nazareth, stand up and walk." And he took him by the right hand and raised him up; and immediately his feet and ankles were made strong. Jumping up, he stood and began to walk, and he entered the temple with them, walking and leaping and praising God.

Ever since the creation of the world his eternal power and divine nature, invisible though they are, have been understood and seen through the things he has made. So they are without excuse.

Material: a frog

Here is our friend the frog again. *(show the frog; this time you may want to pick it up so everyone can see, but don't allow touching by the children because frogs can carry bacteria)* Do you notice something about this frog? He has really big and strong back legs for jumping. When I look at Mr. Frog, I think of a story about a man who got healed back in Bible days. This man was a beggar who sat by the temple gate. He was crippled and he could not walk. One day, when two of Jesus' special helpers (called apostles) saw the man they said, "Look at us." Then the apostles used the name of Jesus to bring healing to the man so he could walk and would not have to beg for money anymore. The Bible tells us that he went running and leaping and praising God. I wonder if that man could leap as well as Mr. Frog?

But I want you to see something else about our frog, too. He has great big eyes, and they are almost on top of his head! *(point these out to the children)* When Mr. Frog is in the muddy pond, he isn't looking at the dirty water around him. His eyes are above the water, looking all around at the beautiful world God has made. The man who needed healing looked at the apostles. They told him about Jesus and then he was healed. Mr. Frog is looking at God's beautiful world. Mr. Frog may not know it, but God's world can tell about Jesus, too. Let's follow their example and look only at things that will teach us about God and Jesus.

Praise Joyfully

Scripture: Psalm 98:4
Make a joyful noise to the Lord, all the earth; break forth into joyous song and sing praises.

Material: a frog, an inflated balloon

I love springtime, don't you, boys and girls? I love it when the grass starts to grow and the flowers come out on the trees. It is my favorite time of year.

I know someone else who likes springtime. Can you guess? It's our friend, Mr. Frog. *(indicate frog)* When spring comes, Mr. Frog finds himself a real nice spot next to the water somewhere and sits himself down. Then he blows his throat up like a balloon *(use balloon to demonstrate how a frog inflates his throat)*, and he sings and he sings and he sings. *(let the air escape from the balloon with a squeaking noise)* Okay, it doesn't sound like that. It sounds more like this. *(imitate a frog sound or two)*

Have you heard the frogs singing? Do you think we should invite them to sing in our church choir? *(have a little comic discussion of what it would be like to have frogs in the choir)*

Okay, well we probably won't have frogs in the choir, then, but we can learn something from Mr. Frog about this. When Mr. Frog decides to sing, he doesn't stare at the floor and barely move his mouth. He doesn't hide behind the frog next to him and be shy. Mr. Frog takes a deep breath and sings right out!

God wants us to be that way when we sing praises to him. He wants us to praise joyfully! He wants to hear a joyful noise!

Butterflies

I do not prefer the commercially supplied painted lady butterfly for my object lesson, simply because its life cycle doesn't fit my four-week schedule. There is a more cooperative subject to be found in the cabbage or white sulphur butterfly, which is available in nature over most of the United States. These are those pretty little white butterflies whose annoying larvae munch everything related to mustard and cabbage from our gardens: cabbage, brussels sprouts, broccoli, and even nasturtiums. It is usually among the nasturtiums that I find my specimens. In fact, I plant nasturtiums for just this reason.

Watch for the pretty, white butterfly that is lighting briefly on one leaf after another. That is probably the mom. She is laying a single egg, or at most two, on each leaf. They are very small, but if you look closely you can see them as a tiny white grain attached to the leaf. Pick these leaves on Saturday afternoon and arrange them in a small container of water like a bouquet. They will hatch in a week, and you will have lovely green butterfly larvae big enough for the children to see in two weeks. Put them in any old jar or clear container with air holes, or you can get fancy and purchase one of those butterfly habitats at the store. Feed them with whatever you found them on ... lots of it.

It gets better. Keep feeding these little fellows and they will grow to become sleepy little chrysalises for the next lesson, then butterflies for the next lesson, and still alive to be released for the fourth lesson. See how cooperative they are?

Does it get any better? Yes! These butterflies are natives. Release them where you live. Again, we love disposable pets.

The Eye Of Faith

Scripture: Hebrews 11:1
Now faith is the assurance of things hoped for, the conviction of things not seen.

Material: a bouquet of nasturtium (or other) leaves with butterfly eggs on them

Do you know what I have here, boys and girls? *(make a big deal of admiring your bouquet)* This is a butterfly bouquet! Isn't it beautiful? *(the children will react; nudge them a little to get someone to say that there are no butterflies)*

What? You don't see any butterflies? Well, I do! You see, I was out in my yard and I saw Momma Butterfly flitting around my garden. *(imitate butterfly, be a little silly)* All of a sudden, I noticed something. Momma Butterfly was stopping here and there to lay little eggs on my plants! The eggs are very, very tiny. You can't even see them from where you are sitting, but they are there. Now, if I just wait, pretty soon some little caterpillars will hatch out, then they will become chrysalises, and then I will have butterflies! So when I look at this bunch of leaves, boys and girls, I don't just see leaves, I see a butterfly garden! Why? Because I have faith that those little eggs will hatch, that's why!

God wants us to have that kind of faith when it comes to believing what he tells us, too. Sometimes we find a promise in God's Word and we think, "Wow, I don't see that!" But you know what? If we believe God's Word — and we already know that God cannot lie — then we will believe in things that we might not be able to see. What kind of things? Oh, things like Jesus, and angels, and the Holy Spirit, and heaven.... Just like I believe that this bunch of leaves will turn into a butterfly garden and I believe that what God has said will happen in my life. Faith means believing when you can't yet see.

Growing By The Word Of God

Scripture: 1 Peter 2:2
Like newborn infants, long for the pure, spiritual milk, so that by it you may grow into salvation.

Material: butterfly larvae that should be large enough to see by now (For purposes of continuity, place them on a fresh bouquet of the same greens you brought before, but keep a few leaves that have obvious chewed spots.)

Well, well, well, what have we here? *(look closely at the bouquet)* I see something crawling around in these leaves. You know what? It looks like my butterfly eggs have hatched out some little caterpillars and they are starting to grow! Last week, we had to have faith and believe that those little butterfly eggs would hatch. Now I have to have faith that these caterpillars will turn into butterflies! They don't look like beautiful butterflies now, but they will some day!

Wow! *(pick up one of the leaves that is partially eaten)* Look at that! These little guys are really hungry. Look how they made holes in this leaf! You know, I've been watching these fellows ever since they hatched, and they only seem to do two things: Eat and grow. Eat and grow. They are feeding *(emphasize that word — it is probably a new one in this context to most of the children)* on these leaves. That is what is making them grow so fast.

We can learn something from these little caterpillars, boys and girls. Just like the caterpillars are feeding on these leaves, we should feed on the Word of God! No, I don't mean we should tear the pages out of our Bibles and eat them. To feed on the Word of God, all we have to do is read it and think about it. Or, if you don't know how to read yet, ask Mom and Dad to read it for you or tell you Bible stories. Just like these baby butterflies grow by feeding on leaves, we can grow in spirit by feeding on the Word of God.

Is He Dead?

Scripture: Matthew 28:7

> *Then go quickly and tell his disciples, "He has been raised from the dead, and indeed he is going ahead of you to Galilee; there you will see him." This is my message for you.*

Material: a container full of chrysalises (After the growing lesson, be sure to put your larvae in a container with a ventilated lid, large enough for all the butterflies to spread their wings when they emerge. By midweek they should have hung themselves from the top edges of the container and formed chrysalises. Do not disturb them. Bring the whole container to class.)

Hello, boys and girls, do you remember the cute little caterpillars I brought last week? We talked about how they were growing and growing by feeding on green leaves, just like we can grow and grow by feeding on the Word of God.

But look at them now! *(peer intently into the container)* They are not feeding anymore. They are not moving anymore. They are all wrapped up in those little bags. Are they dead?

No. The baby butterflies are not dead, boys and girls. They are sleeping, and they are changing. These little sleeping bags are called chrysalises. Inside each of those chrysalises, our little caterpillar friends are changing into butterflies. When they are done changing into butterflies, they will come out. Next week we will be able to see them!

When I see a caterpillar all wrapped up like that, it reminds me of someone very important. It reminds me of Jesus. When Jesus died, they took his body and wrapped it up and put it in a garden tomb. All of his friends thought he was going to stay dead forever, but Jesus did not stay dead. After three days, Jesus took off those wrapping cloths and came walking right out of the cave. Jesus is alive.

Ascending To Heaven

Scripture: Luke 24:51-53
> *While he was blessing them, he withdrew from them and was carried up into heaven. And they worshiped him, and returned to Jerusalem with great joy; and they were continually in the temple blessing God.*

Material: butterflies in a jar (If your butterflies have cooperated, they should be ready to fly by now.)

Okay, boys and girls, what do you think? Our baby butterflies are all grown up! *(show the jar filled with butterflies)* Aren't they beautiful? Remember when they were just little eggs and we could hardly see them? We had to believe that those eggs would hatch, didn't we? We had to believe what we could not see. That's faith!

Then we had caterpillars. Those little guys ate and ate. We learned that the baby butterflies grow by feeding on green leaves, just like we grow by feeding on the Word of God. Did you feed on the Word of God this week, boys and girls? *(let them answer)*

Last week our little friends were chrysalises, wrapped up in their little bags just like Jesus was wrapped up in the garden tomb. But look at them now! Just like Jesus came out of the tomb, our butterflies have come out of their little sleeping bags.

But, boys and girls, do these butterflies belong in this cage? No. They need to fly, don't they? Well, that makes me think of Jesus, too. Probably after Jesus was raised from the dead, his friends wanted him to stay with them forever. But Jesus still had work to do. So, after a few days of visiting with his friends, Jesus ascended into heaven. That big word means that Jesus went up into heaven as his friends watched him and they worshiped God.

Let's let these butterflies go, shall we? And as we watch them go, we will think about Jesus ascending into heaven and we will worship God. *(take the class outside or go to a window to release the butterflies)*

Grass

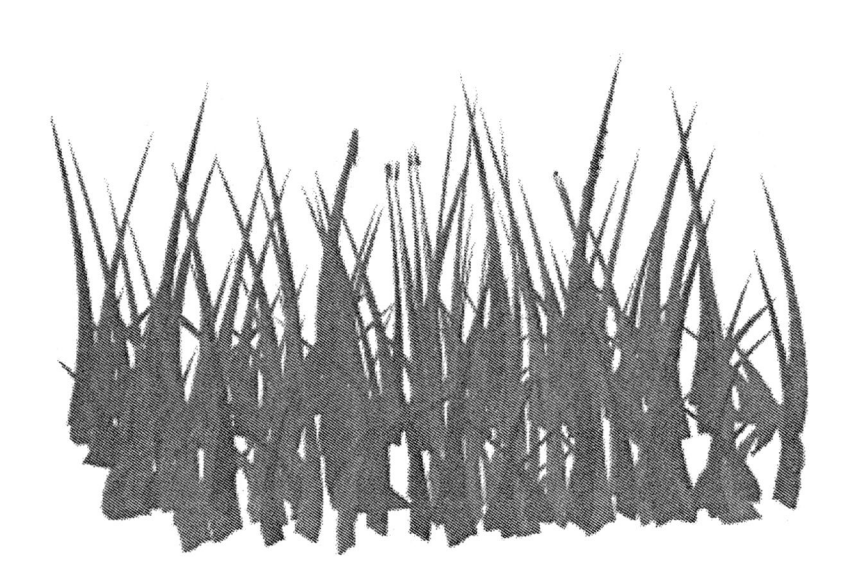

Grass may not be as exciting as frogs and butterflies, but it is alive, and it does lend itself well to object lessons. Jesus used it, didn't he? For this lesson series, you will need to plant one flat of pure grass seed and one flat of grass seed mixed with weeds (wild bird seed works great). Plant your flats a week before you plan to begin the lesson series. They will sprout in seven days, but will not have the lush growth we need for the third lesson unless you prepare in advance.

For the second lesson, leave your planted flats at home and bring materials to plant a flat in front of the children. You can toss this one when you get home because it won't grow fast enough to be of use later. For the third lesson, bring the three-week-old grass flat and the mixed grass and weed flat. Prepare in advance for lesson four by neglecting to water the grass after lesson two.

This lesson seems dull to the adult eye, but you will be surprised how interesting it is to young children. As one child said to me after experiencing this lesson, "I never saw grass before!" I'm sure that is not exactly what was meant, but the response was gratifying, even so.

What Kind Of Soil?

Scripture: Mark 4:3-8

Listen! A sower went out to sow. And as he sowed, some seed fell on the path, and the birds came and ate it up. Other seed fell on rocky ground, where it did not have much soil, and it sprang up quickly, since it had no depth of soil. And when the sun rose, it was scorched; and since it had no root, it withered away. Other seed fell among thorns, and the thorns grew up and choked it, and it yielded no grain. Other seed fell into good soil and brought forth grain, growing up and increasing and yielding thirty and sixty and a hundredfold.

Material: a flat of potting soil, a flat of soil with rocks, a chunk of hard clay dirt, and a thorny branch

(start the lesson by obviously playing with the dirt; laugh and make it look like fun) You know what? I love to play in the dirt. I like to dig. I like to pile the dirt up and make castles. I like to make mud pies. I like to plant things. What do you like to do with dirt? *(let them answer)*

Well, I have a few different kinds of dirt here. I have some potting soil. *(show it)* The potting soil is perfect for plants. It has lots of nutrients, and it's nice and loose so the roots of the plant can move around in there and get food and water. I also have some soil with rocks. *(show it)* Do you think a little plant would like to try to grow up next to this? *(drop a rock to impress the children that it is heavy and not good for plants)* Whoa!

I have another kind of soil, too. It's called clay *(show it)*, and it packs down really hard. I don't think it is very good for plants, do you? I have something here that is not soil; it's a thorny weed. Thorny weeds sometimes choke out the things I plant, and I don't like them.

Jesus said that our hearts are like these kinds of soil. Some hearts are full of thorny weeds. That's not good. *(set the thorn aside)*

Some hearts are hard like clay. That's not good, either. *(set the clay aside)* Some hearts are full of rocks. Not good. *(set aside)* But, some hearts are just right. A heart that is just right for Jesus is a heart that wants to hear his word. It is a heart that wants to do right. Let's have good hearts, and see what Jesus can do in us!

Sowing A Seed

Scripture: Luke 8:11
Now the parable is this: The seed is the word of God.

Material: a flat of soil, grass seeds, and a pitcher of water

Do you know what, boys and girls? In my backyard I have a garden. In the garden, I plant tomato seeds to get tomatoes. I plant radish seeds to get radishes. I plant lettuce seeds to get lettuce. Every seed grows exactly what it was meant to grow. That is the way God planned it. He said that each seed would bear fruit after its own kind.

But today *(indicate your soil and seeds)*, I am planting grass seeds. I have some good, rich soil right here and I have some seeds that came from grass plants, so I know they will grow into grass. *(begin planting as you talk)* I'll just stir my soil up a little here so the little grass seeds can put down some roots. I'll spread the grass seeds around. Did you know that is called "sowing"? It sounds like what you do with a needle and thread, but it's not the same. This is "sowing seeds." I'm going to sow lots and lots of seeds in here so I can have a nice, lush garden of grass. Then I'll pat the soil down over my seeds and add a little water. There! We're done. Now we just have to wait and see what happens to my little garden here.

You know what? God has a garden, too. We are God's garden! Do you know what kind of seed he sows in us? His Word. Whenever we hear the Word of God at church, or Mom and Dad tell us a Bible story ... even when we read the Bible for ourselves ... God is sowing his word into our hearts. God's Word is the seed that makes us grow more and more like Jesus. Let's make sure we let God sow lots of seed in us!

Weeds!

Scripture: Matthew 13:14-20

> *With them indeed is fulfilled the prophecy of Isaiah that says: "You will indeed listen, but never understand, and you will indeed look, but never perceive. For this people's heart has grown dull, and their ears are hard of hearing, and they have shut their eyes; so that they might not look with their eyes, and listen with their ears, and understand with their heart and turn — and I would heal them." But blessed are your eyes, for they see, and your ears, for they hear. Truly I tell you, many prophets and righteous people longed to see what you see, but did not see it, and to hear what you hear, but did not hear it. "Hear then the parable of the sower. When anyone hears the word of the kingdom and does not understand it, the evil one comes and snatches away what is sown in the heart; this is what was sown on the path. As for what was sown on rocky ground, this is the one who hears the word and immediately receives it with joy."*

Material: a flat of pure grass and a flat of mixed grass and weeds

Oh, my goodness, look at this! Boys and girls, I have two gardens here. Which one of them is like the one I planted last week? Well, let's see. *(consider both gardens as you speak)* I know that what I sowed in my garden was grass seed, so let's check out these two gardens. This garden *(indicate grass)* is all grass. So what kind of seed do you think was sown in there? *(let them answer)*

Okay, now what about this other garden? *(indicate the mixed garden)* I see some grass in here, all right. But what's this? *(pull out a weed and look at it)* This is not grass. And what about this? And this? And this? *(pull other weeds with flourish)* Somebody must have put some weed seeds in this garden! But you know what? If I try to pull out all the seeds, my poor little grass plants will get pulled up with them. I'm just going to have to let them all grow together until the grass is stronger. *(set mixed garden aside)* That is messed up.

You know what, boys and girls? The Bible tells us that sometimes the people we know are like that messed-up garden. Some people are growing from the seed of the Word of God. They are becoming more and more like Jesus. But some people are not letting God sow his Word in their hearts. They are letting bad seeds be sown in there. They are not growing to be more like Jesus at all! Let's learn from these two gardens and make sure that we let only the Word of God be sown in our hearts. We don't want to be a messed-up garden!

Water!

Scripture: 1 Corinthians 3:6
I planted, Apollos watered, but God gave growth.

Material: a flat of grass that has been cared for and a flat of grass that has not been watered properly (wilted and turning brown)

Boys and girls, look at this mess! *(show them your wilted grass)* Something terrible has happened to my garden! What could have gone wrong? I know I planted good grass seeds, because grass is what came up. I know I gave the seeds good soil. I patted the soil down. I know I did everything right. What's wrong with my grass? *(if the children are too young to know, prompt a helper to point out that the grass lacks water)*

Water? But I watered it once when I planted it. Isn't that enough? *(let the children respond, then prompt your helper again, if necessary)*

Well, you are right. Grass needs to be watered again and again, not just once. I guess I better take this grass home and give it a big drink of water, shouldn't I?

You know what, boys and girls? This lesson about grass makes me think of something. I watered my grass garden once, but that was not enough. I needed to water it again and again. We are God's garden. He sows his seed in us when we hear the Word of God. But how does God's garden get watered? God's garden gets watered when we hear the same things again and again. The first time we hear a Bible story or a Bible truth, it is like a seed gets planted. Every time we hear that same thing again, it is like God is pouring a little water on that seed. Don't dry up like my grass, boys and girls. Hear the Word of God again and again and let God water you!

Single Sermons

Not everyone teaches in series, or has the opportunity to do so. Here are a few of my favorite "live" object lessons intended for single lesson use.

People often ask me how I choose an animal or object to use for a lesson. When I first began, most of them chose me! I would just come across an animal or insect and an idea for an object lesson would pop into my head. I'm sure it was inspiration from God, because they were so successful. After that, I began looking on purpose, and even purchased creatures for specific lesson ideas. One thing, though, I always teach what I know. If I happen upon a creature about which I know very little, I do a lot of research before I ever take it to a class. Also, I make sure I am comfortable handling the would-be classroom visitor before I take it in front of the children. I don't want to communicate any fear or insecurity to them. If I cannot handle the visitor, I find someone to help me who feels comfortable with it.

How do I obtain my specimens? Nothing could be easier! I make it a point to use only what is readily available (although sometimes seasonal). Most of my classroom visitors can be picked up in the backyard, a vacant lot, or an obliging field or marsh. These include snails, flies, bees, larvae of all sorts, frogs, toads, lizards, snakes ... the list is inexhaustible. Later in this book, I will show you how to turn almost anything you come across into an object lesson. That's when the fun really begins. You will find that God crosses your path with critters that are "just perfect for next week's object lesson" with amazing regularity!

If such is not available to you, become friends with your local bait shop owner. They usually have a ready supply of worms, crayfish, shrimp, minnows, and lots of other things. Many people are happy to donate a critter or two for classroom use. The garden shop of your hardware store is a good source for ladybugs and praying mantises.

Another source of supply is the pet store. I'm not talking about buying pets. Remember, whenever possible, we want our live object lessons to be disposable. I tried to become my own supplier once and my home turned into a zoo. Don't buy pets, buy pet food.

Live foods available at pet stores include superworms, mealworms, silkworms, wax worms, crickets, fish, and mice.

One favorite source for me is friends and neighbors. I find that most people are very happy to either loan out or bring to my class their family pets, farm animals, and exotics. People love to show off their animals! It's part of the fun of ownership. You can even use borrowing an animal as a way to invite a friend to church for the first time.

Most of all, be creative and be bold! My favorite object lesson of all time is one in which we were teaching about boldness. We pretended to perform a surgical operation on one of the classroom helpers and pulled a live chicken from behind the table to demonstrate getting the "chicken" out of us so we can be bold for Jesus. I still hear about that one every time I run into someone who was there. So, get the chicken out and be bold with your live object lessons!

Don't Be Ashamed

Scripture: Luke 12:8-9

And I tell you, everyone who acknowledges me before others, the Son of Man also will acknowledge before the angels of God, but whoever denies me before others will be denied before the angels of God.

Material: a container of ladybugs

(Keep the bugs hidden during the introduction.) I brought a new visitor to class today. Can you guess who it is? I'll give some hints *(Give hints and allow for guesses. Suggested hints: she is small and round; she can fly; she likes to live around rose bushes; she eats aphids; and she is red and has black spots.)* Very good! You guessed it. Our special guest today is a ladybug. *(bring out your container of ladybugs)*

Ladybugs are one of my favorite insects. They sure are pretty, aren't they?

Now you know, some insects are the color of the plants they live on. They are green or brown or gray. This helps them to hide from predators. That big word, "predator," means other animals want to eat them for lunch! But the ladybug is not afraid to show off her pretty, red color. She is not ashamed. Do you know why? Ladybugs taste terrible! Their pretty, red color is like a stop sign to predators: "Stop! Don't eat that!"

You know what? We can learn something from the ladybug. Just like she is not ashamed to wear her bright, red color, we should not be ashamed to wear the name of Jesus. Jesus said that if we were ashamed of him, he would be ashamed of us. But if we are bold and brave about Jesus like the ladybug is bold and brave about her red color, then he will be proud to say that he knows us. Let's make Jesus proud! Don't be ashamed!

The Armor Of God

Scripture: Ephesians 6:14-17

Stand therefore, and fasten the belt of truth around your waist, and put on the breastplate of righteousness. As shoes for your feet put on whatever will make you ready to proclaim the gospel of peace. With all of these, take the shield of faith, with which you will be able to quench all the flaming arrows of the evil one. Take the helmet of salvation, and the sword of the Spirit, which is the word of God.

Material: pill bugs (aka roly-polies, sow bugs) in a container that allows viewing

Look what I have today. Pill bugs! Aren't they cute? *(If your group is small, this is a good time to spill the pill bugs out on a piece of paper. Draw a circle around them and let them "race" to see who gets out of the circle first.)*

Pill bugs live in damp places, like under rocks and logs. They eat dead plants and anything that is rotting. In fact, they are some of God's recyclers. We call them pill bugs because they roll up in little balls if they are in danger. This protects their soft bodies by wrapping the outside shells around them. *(encourage a pill bug to demonstrate by poking it with a finger)* It makes them look like a pill, so they earned the name "pill bug," get it? But did you know that pill bugs are not really bugs at all? They are crustaceans, like crabs and lobsters. I think that is amazing!

When I was growing up, we used to call these funny little creatures armor bugs because they looked like flat, little knights in shining armor. Whenever I see them, I remember to put on the whole armor of God.

What is the armor of God? Well, the Bible tells us that we have an enemy called the devil. So God gave us special invisible armor to keep us safe. This armor is made of powerful spiritual things like truth, righteousness, peace, faith, salvation, and the Word of

God. We might not understand it all, but that won't keep it from working! God says we can wear his armor, so I'm wearing it! How do I put on this invisible armor? I just say, "I am putting on the whole armor of God. Just like it says in the Bible."

Pray, Pray, Pray

Scripture: 1 Thessalonians 5:17
... pray without ceasing ...

Material: a praying mantis (It is really cool if you can hold this and let it crawl around your hand, but it does jump, so be careful ... also, try to get one without big wings so it won't fly away.)

Did you ever see a praying mantis catch a bug? It's awesome! The mantis sits on a stick or on the side of the wall. He has kind of a little hook on his feet so he can hold on tightly. He waits and he waits. Pretty soon, all the bugs have forgotten that he came there. They think he is just part of the scenery! Then a bug comes strolling along *(stroll and hum)*, and *wham!* — that praying mantis grabs Mr. Bug with his powerful front legs and has him for lunch.

Praying mantises are very welcome visitors in our gardens because they eat a lot of harmful insects. But, look at this beautiful praying mantis. When I see him with his arms folded, it reminds me that I should pray. And, when I see him sitting still like that for a long time, it reminds me that I should pray *a lot!*

Prayer is just talking to God. There are lots of different ways to pray. Sometimes we are asking God for something. Sometimes we are thanking him for what he has already done. Worshiping is another kind of prayer, and it is prayer when we tell God that we will do whatever he wants us to do. Pastors pray. Moms and Dads pray. Children pray. Anyone can pray. Prayer is just talking to God, and you can talk to God about anything you want. He cares about you.

Walk In The Light

Scripture: 1 John 1:7
... but if we walk in the light as he himself is in the light, we have fellowship with one another, and the blood of Jesus his Son cleanses us from all sin.

Material: earthworms (night crawlers are best because they are big)

Here are our special guests today. I brought lots of them: earthworms! *(laugh and let a handful of worms slide between your fingers ... the children will react)* I love worms! Worms are cool! Do you know why earthworms are cool! Earthworms make dirt.

It's true! Earthworms crawl along, eating anything that is rotten. It goes all the way through their long, long bodies, and it comes out as dirt! Really good dirt, too! Not only that, worms also dig holes, which help air and water get down into the ground so our gardens can grow better. Everyone should have lots of busy earthworms in their gardens.

Earthworms live almost their whole lives in the dark. Even if they are not under the ground, they hide under rocks and grass and wood. Earthworms do not like the light at all. In fact, they don't even have eyes to see with! You will never find an earthworm lying out on the beach wearing sunglasses!

God does not want us to be like earthworms. He does not want us to live in spiritual darkness. The Bible says that God's Word is light. If we listen to the Word of God; if we read the Bible or ask Mom and Dad to read it to us, we will get that light inside us. That light will help us to know what to do and where to go every day. It will teach us the difference between right and wrong. It will make us more like Jesus.

Don't be like a blind, old earthworm hiding in the dark. Walk with Jesus. Walk in the light!

Hold On To The Good

Scripture: 1 Thessalonians 5:21
   ... but test everything; hold fast to what is good.

Material: crayfish

Does anybody know what this is? It looks like a baby lobster, but it is really a crayfish. Some people would say, "crawdad."

Lobsters, you know, live in the ocean where the water is salty. Crayfish live in creeks and even rivers and ponds where the water is fresh, or not salty. Crayfish like to hide down on the bottom of the stream, under rocks and roots of trees. They wait in their little hiding places until a fish or a tadpole comes by and then, *whoosh!* They jump out of hiding and grab their dinner with this big claw. *(indicate large claw)* Crayfish also eat worms and bugs ... or anything that is dead in the water.

Crayfish are also good to eat. In some places, people have big parties and cook lots and lots of crayfish in many different recipes. Big fish like to eat them, too. You can use a crayfish on your hook to go fishing.

The thing I notice most about our crayfish is his big claw. I don't want to put my finger in the water because I am sure he will pinch me. I have seen this crayfish grab a little stick and hold it. But when he tests it and finds out it is not good food, he lets it go. When he finds something to eat, though, he grabs it with his claw and holds on tight.

We can learn from the crayfish. When we find something that is not good for us, we should let it go right away. But when we find something good, hold on tightly. That's what God wants us to do!

Run!

Scripture: Hebrews 12:1
Therefore, since we are surrounded by so great a cloud of witnesses, let us also lay aside every weight and the sin that clings so closely, and let us run with perseverance the race that is set before us.

Material: millipedes

Whoa, check these guys out! Did you ever see so many legs? *(It is perfectly safe to let a millipede run all over your hands and arms. I have even put one on my nose to get a laugh. A cooperative child can hold one, too. Wash your hands afterward. Millipedes are not germy, but they can leave a funny smell if they get nervous.)*

These are millipedes. "Millipede" is a word that means 1,000 legs or 1,000 feet, but they don't really have that many. The biggest millipedes only have about 200 legs ... but I think that is plenty. It is a good thing millipedes don't wear shoes. I would hate to have to help them tie their shoelaces!

Millipedes are recyclers like snails and pill bugs. They live in damp places and eat dead plants and things like that. Millipedes are not harmful to humans. They don't bite. Don't mix them up with centipedes, though. Centipedes do bite. *(It is a good idea to show a picture of a centipede so the children can tell the difference. Verbal descriptions don't mean much to children.)* You can tell the difference because centipedes are flatter with longer legs, and they don't have as many legs as millipedes do.

When I see a millipede going across the floor, it makes me think of running. Those little legs can really go! The Bible says that living for Jesus is like running a race. To run our race, we need to love God and love people. We need to be kind and give when someone has a need. We need to be at church and worship God. If we do these things, we will run a good race.

We might not have as many legs as a millipede, but we can run a good race for Jesus, can't we?

Superman!

Scripture: Philippians 4:13
I can do all things through him who strengthens me.

Material: a carton of superworms (Note: superworms are very fast movers, so it is quite spectacular when you dump them out onto a surface for the children to see. Enjoy the reaction!)

I have a really cool bunch of friends to share with you today, boys and girls. Superworms! *(dump the carton)* Look at those guys go! Did you know that superworms can move as fast backward as they do forward! I wonder if I can do that? *(try it)* Okay, well, maybe not.

Superworms are actually baby beetles. The mother beetle lays her eggs in grain and when the little larvae come out, they start eating. The babies grow, but their skins don't grow with them. When they get too big for their skin, they just *pop* it off and there is a brand new skin right underneath. Isn't that amazing? Then, one day the skin of the superworm starts to turn hard, and he goes to sleep inside it for a few days. When the hard skin pops off ... *wow!* Superworm is a super beetle!

When I look at these superworms, I remember that God has made me super, too. I may not look like it, but I am a superman! And guess what? You are a superman, too!

How do I know? Because Jesus lives inside me, that's how. I asked him to come and live in my heart and he did. So, now when I need to do something, it isn't just me doing it. Jesus is in here *(point to self)* helping me all the way.

These are not ordinary worms, they are superworms. And you are not ordinary, either. You are *super!*

Don't Be Lukewarm

Scripture: Revelation 3:16
So, because you are lukewarm, and neither cold nor hot, I am about to spit you out of my mouth.

Material: a lizard (any lizard will do, it doesn't have to be anything fancy, but bigger is always better) and a dime

Our visitor in class today is a lizard. *(explain what kind of lizard, how you come to have it, some of its habits, and the like)* Lizards come in all different shapes and sizes. Did you know that the world's smallest lizard is so small that a full-grown one can curl up and take a nap on a dime? *(show dime)* And the world's largest lizard, the Komodo dragon, can weigh up to 300 pounds! Some lizards eat plants. Some lizards eat meat. Some lizards eat both! Some lizards are good swimmers. Some lizards live in the desert and never see any more water than the dew on a blade of grass. Some lizards are gray and brown and can hide in sand and rocks and trees. Other lizards have bright and flashy colors that make you notice them wherever they are.

But there is one thing all lizards have in common. Lizards cannot keep themselves warm. They are what we call "cold-blooded." Lizards have to lay out in the sun, or find some other source of heat, to keep their bodies from getting so cold that they just go to sleep or even die. As a lizard cools off, he moves slower and slower. A lizard can't do much when he is only lukewarm. Lizards need to stay hot!

When I see a lizard, it reminds me that I need to stay hot, too. I need to stay hot for Jesus! If I don't hear the Word of God and worship him and stay around my good Christian friends, I might become a lukewarm Christian. And a Christian can't do much when he is lukewarm.

Under His Shadow

Scripture: Matthew 23:37
> *Jerusalem, Jerusalem, the city that kills the prophets and stones those who are sent to it! How often have I desired to gather your children together as a hen gathers her brood under her wings, and you were not willing!*

Material: a clutch of chicks (Borrow these — they are not disposable. For showing them, I recommend a wire cage or an old aquarium. Cover it to begin the lesson.) *Note: a box of antibacterial wipes should be on hand for those children who touch the chicks, to avoid any potential diseases.

Listen, boys and girls. Do you hear something? *(listen intently)* I have our classroom visitors under this cover. Can you guess who they are? *(allow time for guessing and then uncover the chicks)* You are right. I brought some little, baby chickens to class this morning! *(talk about the chicks: how old they are and where you got them)*

Now, these chicks, like all chicks, were hatched from eggs. If we were out on the farm, the mother hen would have been sitting on her eggs. Then, when the chicks hatched out, she would have taught them how to scratch in the dirt for food *(imitate)*, how to drink water from a dish or a puddle *(imitate)*, and all sorts of other things. But the most important thing the mother hen would teach these chicks is this: how to stay warm and safe.

The mother hen has a special place where her chicks will always be warm and safe. Do you know where that place is? It is under her wings. She clucks a special cluck and all the little chicks come running. Then she ruffles up her feathers and the little chicks snuggle up next to her softest place; right under the shadow of those wings.

God wants to be like a mother hen to us, boys and girls. He calls us every day and he wants us to come running. God wants us to stay close to him, snuggled in the shadow of his wings.

Sweet Like Honey

Scripture: Psalm 19:10
More to be desired are they than gold, even much fine gold; sweeter also than honey, and drippings of the honeycomb.

Material: a jar with several honeybees inside it and a Bible

Our visitors today are these little honeybees. I found them *(tell the when, where, and how)* and brought them to our class for you to see. A lot of people are afraid of bees because of their sting, but most bees are actually pretty calm and will only sting you if you step on them, swat at them, or frighten them in some way. The stinger is for their protection.

Bees are very important to us. They live in hives with hundreds of other bees and they are very busy creatures. Bees fly around looking for flowers. When they find some, they go back to the hive and tell their friends where the flowers are. Then the bees go to the flowers and collect the nectar and pollen. Nectar is the sweet juice of the flower. Pollen is a special kind of dust that flowers make. Some of the pollen falls off onto other flowers as the bees fly around. This is very good for the plants.

Do you know why the bees are doing all this? They are making honey! Back at the hive, they make honey from the sweet nectar they have collected. They store it in wax containers called a honeycomb. Honey is very sweet, and it is good for us. The more you eat it, the more you want.

I know something else that is like honey. It is good for us, too. Can you guess what it is? *(indicate Bible)* That's right. It's God's Word. God's Word is good for us. It gives us life and energy. It helps our spirits grow. And the more time we spend reading and listening to God's Word, the more we want. God's Word is sweet like honey.

Hearing The Voice Of God

Scripture: Matthew 11:15
Let anyone with ears listen!

Material: a puppy (definitely borrow this!)

Awww, look! It's a puppy! Boys and girls, this is.... *(tell them about the puppy: its name, where you got it, what kind of a dog it is, and how old it is)*

Dogs have been friends with people for a long time. People had dogs even back in the Bible days. Sometimes the dog is called "man's best friend." Dogs can learn how to do all kinds of things. Dogs can learn to herd sheep and cattle. They can do tricks like fetching things and jumping through hoops. Dogs can learn how to guard things, and can even be police officers and soldiers. How can they do all these things? Dogs can do all these things because they first learned to listen and obey.

When this little puppy was born, his ears were all folded over and he could hardly hear at all. Then, after a few days, he began to hear better and he learned to recognize his mother's sounds and the sounds his brothers and sisters make. Now he knows his master's voice ... and soon he will be able to tell one word from another. After that, he can figure out some of the things we are asking him to do. He will be able to listen and obey.

This little puppy reminds me that we don't know how to listen to God and obey his Word when we first ask Jesus to come into our hearts. We have to grow. We have to learn. Just like this little puppy, we learn how to recognize God's voice and figure out some of the things he is asking us to do. We learn to listen and obey.

Hang In There

Scripture: Proverbs 24:16
... for though they fall seven times, they will rise again; but the wicked are overthrown by calamity.

Material: a jumping spider in a container (they really do jump!)

Do you guys remember the story of Little Miss Muffet? Let's say it together: "Little Miss Muffet sat on a tuffet, eating her curds and whey. Along came a spider who sat down beside her and frightened Miss Muffet away." Well, I don't want anyone to be frightened away, but I did bring a spider today. *(show spider)* Don't be afraid. This is a cute, little jumping spider and he is very friendly.

Now, this little jumping spider has a special talent. He crawls along plants and walls, and even ceilings, looking for tasty bugs. And if he happens to fall, *swish*, he shoots out a line of web as quick as you please to keep himself from hitting the ground, just like Spiderman. He never seems to run out of web. If he falls once ... *swish*. If he falls twice ... *swish, swish*. If he falls seven times ... *swish, swish, swish, swish, swish, swish, swish. (act this out a little)* No matter how many times this little spider falls, he keeps shooting out a web and getting back up again.

We can learn from this little jumping spider, boys and girls. The Bible says that if a good person falls down, he should get up again. God does not mean that if we fall down and really hurt ourselves, that we should get up from that. He means if we make a mistake, or if we fail when we are trying to listen and obey. No matter how many times we fall, no matter how many mistakes we make, no matter how many times we fail ... God wants us to keep getting up, just like this little web-slinger!

Other Objects

Sometimes a live visitor is not readily available, or sometimes I am just too lazy to go dig one up. (If you have read my object lessons up to this point, you know that digging them up is a real possibility!) When those times happen, I resort to using other natural objects and science experiments to make my point. Science is not the enemy of the believer. It is a marvelous tool for teaching an open mind the truths of God's Word.

In Him

Scripture: John 17:21
> ... that all may be one. As you, Father, are in me and I am in you, may they also be in us, so that the world may believe that you have sent me.

Material: a sponge and a clear-sided container filled with enough water to completely cover the sponge

Let's see what I have here today. I have a container. And what is the container full of? *(let the children answer)* That's right, water. I also have a sponge. *(show the sponge)* Now, what do you think is the best thing about a sponge? *(briefly talk about the sponge and then hold it over the container)*

Okay, boys and girls, is this sponge in the water or out of the water? *(wait for the answer, "Out," then put the sponge in the water)* How about now? Is the sponge in the water or out of the water? *(wait for the answer, "In")* Okay, so my sponge is in that water, right? Good.

(lift the water-soaked sponge out of the water, but do not squeeze it) Okay, what about now? Is the sponge in the water? *(wait for the answer, "No")* Good. Okay now. Here comes a hard one: Is the water in the sponge? *(Let them talk about it. The answer is, "Yes," or "Some of it is," but there should be some discussion here. You can repeat the whole exercise again at this point, emphasizing that the sponge is in the water and the water is in the sponge.)*

That is how it is with God, boys and girls. We are in him *(put the sponge in the water)* ... and he is in us. *(lift the sponge and squeeze it to show that there is water in the sponge)* That is what Jesus is talking about in John 17:21 when he says, "Father, I pray that all people who believe in me can be one. You are in me and I am in you."

You know what else? The Bible says that when people see us full of God like this *(dip the sponge and squeeze it out again)*, they

73

will know that God loves us just the same as he loved Jesus. Then, maybe they will want to get in there with us, too *(drop the sponge into the water with a flourish)*, and we can all be one in him.

What Are You Building?

Scripture: 1 Timothy 5:25
So also good works are conspicuous; and even when they are not, they cannot remain hidden.

Material: a bird nest, a teaspoon, some sticks, bits of feathers, and string

I brought something very interesting for you to see today, boys and girls. It's a bird nest *(discuss the nest: where you found it, what sort of bird built it, and so on)*

Bird nests come in all different sizes. Most songbird nests will fit in the palm of your hand, but an eagle's nest is big enough for one of you to sit in. A hummingbird's nest will fit in a teaspoon. *(show teaspoon)*

Birds build their nests in lots of different places. Eagles like to put their nests in high trees or on mountain ledges. Robins and mockingbirds like trees and bushes. Some birds lay their eggs in a shallow, little, scraped-out spot on the ground.

Different birds use different materials to build their nests. Some birds use sticks and bits of feathers and string. *(have some of these materials to show as you talk)* Others build their nests of mud. Some birds build nests that are neat and tidy. Other birds just throw something together. Some birds don't build a nest at all, but lay their eggs in other bird's nests. Every kind of bird builds its own kind of nest. You could study these and then you could look at a nest and say, "I know what kind of bird built that nest!"

Our lives are like a bird's nest in one way. You can tell what kind of people we are by the things we do. We might not be building a nest, but each one of us does things in a certain way. Are we selfish or do we share? Are we kind or do we hurt others on purpose? Are we honest or do we lie?

Let's build our lives so that anyone can look at what we do and then say, "That life was built by someone who loves Jesus. That life was built by a Christian!"

God Looks At The Heart

Scripture: 1 Samuel 16:7
> *But the Lord said to Samuel, "Do not look on his appearance or on the height of his stature, because I have rejected him; for the Lord does not see as mortals see; they look on the outward appearance, but the Lord looks on the heart."*

Material: seven clam shells and one abalone shell, all about the same size

When God sent the prophet, Samuel, to anoint a king for Israel, he sent him to the house of a man named Jesse. God told Samuel that he had chosen one of Jesse's sons to be the king. When Samuel arrived at Jesse's house, he saw that Jesse had eight sons. Let's pretend that these shells are those sons. *(count out the clam shells and abalone shell with the children)*
    Samuel looked at the first son. *(hold up the first clam shell)* His name was Eliab, and he was tall and good looking, so Samuel thought, "My, what a handsome fellow! This must be the one the Lord wants for king of Israel." But God said, "No." *(set the shell down)* Samuel looked at his next son. His name was Abinadab. *(hold up the second clam shell and take a moment to examine it closely, but be sure to look only at the outside of the shell)* "This one is also a very fine looking young man," he thought. "Surely the Lord has chosen this one." But the Lord said, "No." *(put the second shell down)* The third son's name was Shammah. *(pick up the third shell and examine it)* But, guess what? God didn't choose Shammah, either. *(put the shell down, sigh, and shake your head)*
    Samuel looked at seven of Jesse's sons. *(Hold up each of the clam shells in turn. Engage the children with questions like, "Do you think he chose this one?" or "How about this one?" Reject each shell and put it down.)*
    Finally, Samuel looked at Jesse and said, "Don't you have any more sons? The Lord has not chosen any of these."

Jesse answered that he had one more son, the youngest. This son was out watching the sheep. Samuel gave orders to send for the youngest son, whose name was David. *(pick up the abalone shell and examine it, but be sure to show and look at only the outside)* Samuel looked at David, and he didn't see anything special about him, but God said, "Yes, he is the one."

You see, God could see something about David that Samuel could not see. Samuel was looking on the outside. *(show the outside of the shell again)* But God *(turn the shell around so the children can see the beautiful inside of the abalone shell)* looks at the heart.

This outside part of us *(indicate your own body)*, boys and girls, is only a shell. We clean it and dress it up, and make it look as good as we can. But the important things, the things God cares about *(show the inside of the abalone shell again)* are the things on the inside. This shell is from a creature called an abalone. It lives at the bottom of the ocean where we would never see it unless we grabbed it and brought it up. If you looked at this abalone in the water, you would just see this kind of rough and ugly shell. But on the inside, it is smooth and pearly and beautiful. What are you like on the inside? Is your heart full of love or hate? Joy and happiness or ugliness and meanness? God knows. God looks in your heart.

Conclusion

Thank you for sharing this time with me. I hope my object lessons will encourage and inspire you, not just to share God's Word with children through the wonders of nature, but to look at both the natural world and the Word of God in a fresh way ... with childlike faith and enthusiasm.

CPSIA information can be obtained
at www.ICGtesting.com
Printed in the USA
FFOW01n0121110615
14012FF